CAMDENMAINE
BELFAST TO PORT CLYDE

A PHOTOGRAPHIC PORTRAIT

BELFAST

LINCOLNVILLE

ROCKPORT

ROCKLAND

OWLS HEAD

SPRUCE HEAD

PORT CLYDE

MATINICUS ISLAND

MONHEGAN ISLAND

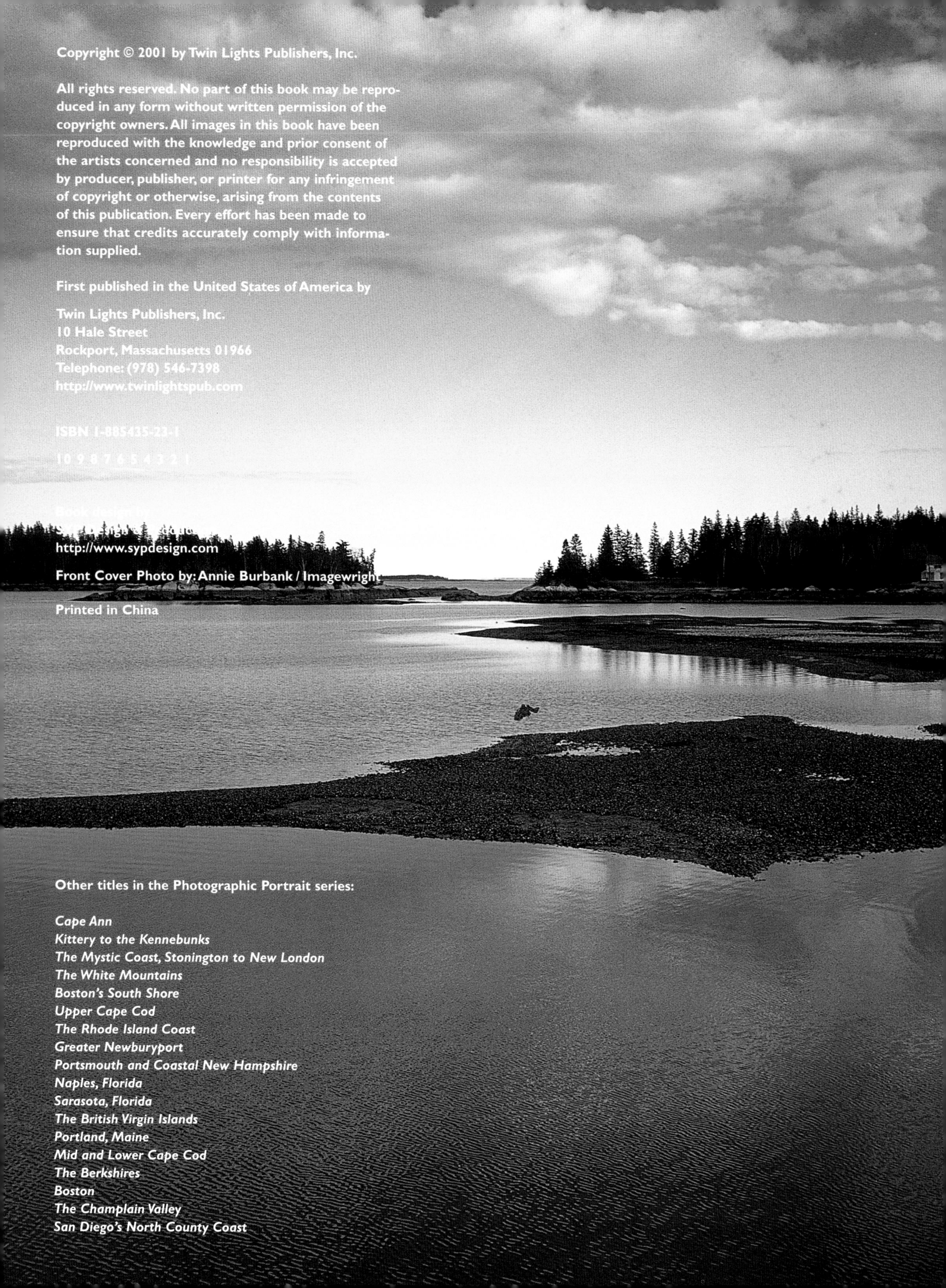

First published in the United States of America by

Twin Lights Publishers, Inc.
10 Hale Street
Rockport, Massachusetts 01966
Telephone: (978) 546-7398
http://www.twinlightspub.com

ISBN 1-885435-23-1

10 9 8 7 6 5 4 3 2 1

Book design by
SYP Design & Production
http://www.sypdesign.com

Front Cover Photo by: Annie Burbank / Imagewright

Printed in China

Other titles in the Photographic Portrait series:

Cape Ann
Kittery to the Kennebunks
The Mystic Coast, Stonington to New London
The White Mountains
Boston's South Shore
Upper Cape Cod
The Rhode Island Coast
Greater Newburyport
Portsmouth and Coastal New Hampshire
Naples, Florida
Sarasota, Florida
The British Virgin Islands
Portland, Maine
Mid and Lower Cape Cod
The Berkshires
Boston
The Champlain Valley
San Diego's North County Coast

TABLE OF CONTENTS

ACKNOWLEDGMENT

Twin Lights Publishers wish to thank all of the photographers who submitted their work for our consideration. Because of space limitations, we were unable to include many excellent photographs in *Camden, Maine– Belfast to Port Clyde: A Photographic Portrait.* The Camden area is a fertile area for many talented resident professional and amateur photographers. The natural beauty attracts visitors to record its special qualities at all times of the year.

We extend our appreciation to Rockport Publishers Inc. of 33 Commercial Street, Gloucester, MA 01930 for providing the aerial photographs.

We are grateful to Bob Moorehead who has written the captions for the photographs in *Camden, Maine–Belfast to Port Clyde: A Photographic Portrait.* He has found evocative titles and added facts to bring out the history and local color for each photograph. We think he as given an added dimension to the book.

And finally, a warm thank you to designer Sara Day of SYP Design & Production for the creation and arrangement of a book that captures the essence of the Camden, Maine area.

This is a book whose heart lies within the towns of Camden and Rockport, their neighboring towns: Rockland, Belfast, Lincolnville and the villages from Owls Head to Port Clyde on the western shore of Maine's Penobscot Bay. It also includes the islands of North Haven, Vinalhaven, Monhegan and Martinicus.

It is many pictures, literally. But it is only a partial picture of a many-faceted geographic treasure—a place steeped in the traditions of its seafarers, its early settlers and in the earliest history of the European conquest of the North American continent.

Penobscot Bay is nearly dead center on the Maine coast—a triangle with a corner pointing at the mouth of the great river that feeds it and bestows its name. The outer tips of the bay are Monhegan Island to the southwest and Isle Au Haut to the northeast.

Within the triangle lies an archipelego that is remote and isolated, where weather is of more than passing interest, where the sea can provide a living as well as take a life, and where self-reliance can be the same as salvation.

It is 35 miles from Port Clyde to Belfast—in a straight line. The distance is doubled in a boat, going in and out of coves and harbors and around islands. Extend the line 11 miles south to Monhegan, then across another 35 miles of sea to Isle Au Haut. From there, point NNW to Belfast.

The Bay, its coastline and its islands, have been fought over by three nations as well as the original native American. It has provided great wooden ships and the men to sail them, and has been an avenue of resources such as, lumber, granite, lime and ice for the world.

Robert Thorndike arrived in Camden Harbor in 1768, journeying from Falmouth (Portland), seeking ash for ships' blocks. He built a house and spent the winter here. The following year, James Richards of Bristol and Dover, N.H. erected a cabin on land bound by what was to be Camden's Free, Washington, Elm and Mechanic streets. His son, James, Jr., later married Mehitable Thorndike, the first white child born in Camden.

In 1791, Peter Ott's Tavern served the "Plantation of Cambden" as a forum for the first town meeting. That same year, William McClathry opened a shipyard and launched the 26-ton sloop "Industry." The population in 1810 was 1,600.

The War of 1812, known locally as "The Sailors' War," marked hard times on the Maine coast. The waters became a hot bed of hit-and-run clashes between American and British privateers and merchantmen.

The British occupied Castine across the Bay, burned a fort at Broad Cove on the St. George River, and raided Northport and Glen Cove (then called Clam Cove). They demanded $80,000 as ransom to keep from burning Camden. The demand was unmet. The town was spared. Further down the coast, Falmouth (Portland) was bombarded.

By 1823, the steamboat "Maine," connected Camden to Bath, and the "Patent" provided steamboat service from Bath to Boston. There were 17 stores in Camden, 16 of which sold liquor.

Shipbuilding was becoming the foundation of the local economy. Joseph (Deacon) Stetson took over the Noah Brooks yard and built 70 vessels in the next 30 years. During the 1830s and 1840s, ship builders were the area's largest employers. Master builder John Pascals was on the way to building 62 ships before he called it a career. Goose River changed its name to Rockport in 1852. Ice was being shipped from Rockport and Camden to ports around the world. In 1860, more than 100 ships carried "Camden, Maine" as their port of hail.

Starting in 1875 and over the next two decades, the Eaton Point Yard turned out 70 ships, inluding 17 three-masters, 24 four-masters, 12 five-masters, and the first six-master, the "George W. Wells." The largest four-master ever built in Penobscot Bay, the 2,628 ton "Frederick Billings," was launched at Rockport in 1885. It was lost off Chile in 1893.

As the nineteenth century edged toward conclusion, things began to change around Penobscot Bay. Camden and Rockport officially separated in 1891, Camden getting the mountains and the beach. In 1892, a great fire swept Camden's business district. The same thing happened to Rockport in 1907. In rebuilding, many merchants decided to use bricks. The lime kilns were banked and the granite trade was closing down. The "Addison E. Bullard," a 1,485 ton schooner, was completed at Rockport in 1904. It was the town's last commercial ship.

In 1900, a steamboat from Boston to Camden could cover the 173 miles in 13 hours. People could reach Boston by train from anywhere in the country. People did—especially "rusticators" from Chicago and Philadelphia.

The rusticators, as the summer folk were first known, built expansive (and expensive) "cottages" and generally moved their families to the Maine coast for the entire summer. They entertained each other lavishly, formed golf clubs and social clubs, and purchased sizable tracts of the best property for development. They built mansions on Ogier Hill and Ogier Point, Beauchamp Point and Melvin Heights, to name a few. The Honorable J. B. Stearns started building a stone castle on 30 acres of shore land on the Belfast Road, a landmark he christened "Norumbega."

Among the rusticator creations was the Mt. Battie Association, which bought 60 acres at the top of the Mt. Battie, built a carriage road to the top and erected a clubhouse. The clubhouse had a view of the entire bay on one side, of Lake Megunticook and the mountains on the other. In 1904, the only local person among the association officers was J.H. Ogier, publisher of the Camden Herald (whose ancestor arrived in the late 1700s). The other officers were from New York, Philadelphia, Chicago and Boston.

The rusticators also came by yacht, privately-owned, ego-extenders, large, ornate and crewed. Today, the standard set by these early recreational sailors has evolved upward and downward on the scales of size, function and formidibility.

Camden's poet laureate is Edna St. Vincent Millay, who spent her youth on these same shores. She evokes a picture of her home in the opening lines of a poem about Camden and the Maine coast:

All I could see from where I stood
was three long mountains and a wood;
I turned and looked the other way,
And saw three islands in the bay,
So with my eyes I traced a line
Of the horizon, thin and fine
Straight around till I was come
Back to where I'd started from;
And all I saw from where I stood,
Was three long mountains and a wood,
Over these things I could not see:
These were the things that bounded me.

At times, the act of artistry fused by camera, film and photographer's eye produces the same range of poetic images. A picture suggests a story. Examine this landscape, the picture requires of the viewer. Those rocks are where they were when the first Europeans cruised these shores. This is where the settler's cabin stood, where the boat was docked. Downeasters aboard China Trade clippers used those same lighthouses to steer their way home. That mansion belonged to the millionaire rusticator who...

On Penobscot Bay, today's photo could be a glimpse at the way things appeared 200 years ago. It could be the same photo taken at some distant point in the future. Like poetry, a photograph only requires a little imagination.

Jammin' Again

ANNIE BURBANK/IMAGEWRIGHT
LEICA M2, FUJI VELVIA

The Windjammer fleet prepares to leave Camden Harbor for another day on the Bay.

Annie Burbank has been photographing for 15 years. Her business, Imagewright, (www.imagewright.com) located in Camden, Maine, includes the whole range of imaging from corporate, portrait, wedding, and stock photography to digital imagery and design. She and her husband, Richard and daughter, Cecile, along with their Portuguese Water Dog, Madeira, live in Tenants Harbor, Maine.

SECOND PRIZE *(opposite)*

Hikers' Haven

PAULA JEAN LUNT
CANON EOS A-2

Black Head, one of three promotories rising 80 to 165 feet on the east side of Monhegan, is a favorite destination of hikers during the summer. The others are White Head and Burnt Head. The island is only 1.75 miles long and about three-quarters of a mile wide, making it an easy walk for most visitors. Hikers are cautioned to keep the breakers at a distances. People have been swept from the rocks with little or no possibility of rescue.

For twenty years Paula Jean Lunt has been photographing the beauty of Maine. A native of Tenants Harbor, ME, Paula started photographing in high school and went on to obtain a degree in photography from the University of Maine and The Maine Photographic Workshops. For 10 years, Paula has run Lunt Studio, photographing portraits and weddings. Today Paula has given up the studio and prefers to photograph outside. Her work can be seen in various travel brochures, magazines and advertisements. When not photographing, Paula goes lobstering and enjoys spending time with her husband and son.

THIRD PRIZE *(above)*

...And Bring A Pail

DEBORAH MURREN
NIKON 8008S, FUJI VELVIA

A dinghy at Spruce Harbor appears out of business until the "hand pump" can be located.

Deborah Murren is a native of West Springfield, Massachusetts and has been making photographs for over 20 years. She has participated in numerous photography classes and workshops and is a member of the Charlottesville Camera Club. She discovered the beauty and charm of the Camden area while attending the Maine Photographic Workshops in Rockport. Deborah currently resides in Albemarle County, Virginia. She is a family nurse practitioner at the University of Virginia Student Health Center in Charlottesville.

As with many colonial towns in New England, the First Congregational Church in Belfast was among the first buildings constructed. Completed in 1765, its tower is visible from all over northern Penobscot Bay and is a critical landmark on many old charts.

Belfast Bay and the Passagassawaukeaq River. Belfast's harbor, once fallen on hard times, has been revived in recent years and now regularly attracts yachtsmen to upper Penobscot Bay.

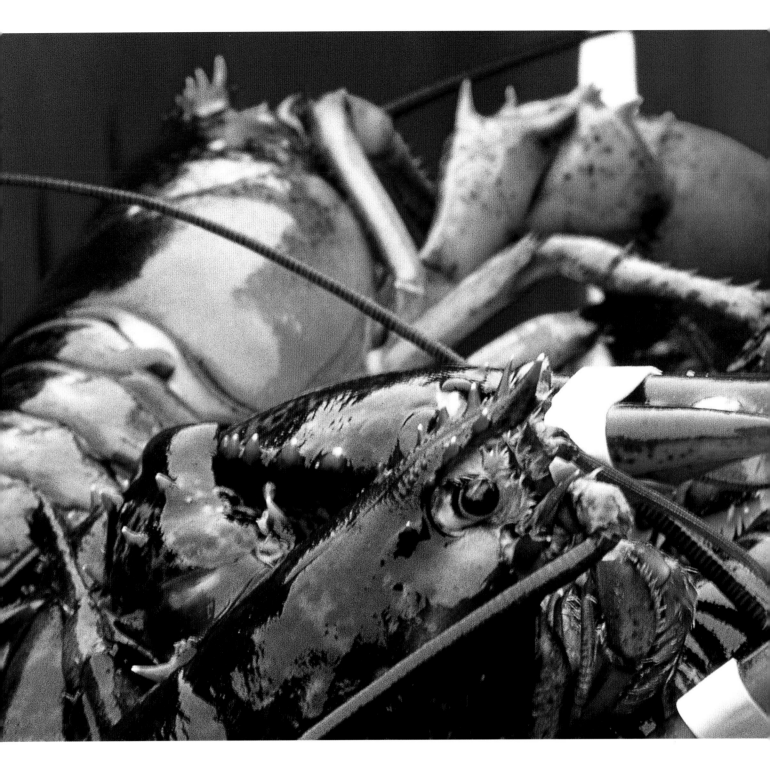

Pot Luck

DEBORAH MURREN
NIKON FM, NIKKOR 105MM, FUJI FILM

Fresh lobsters are on the dock and
ready for the pot.

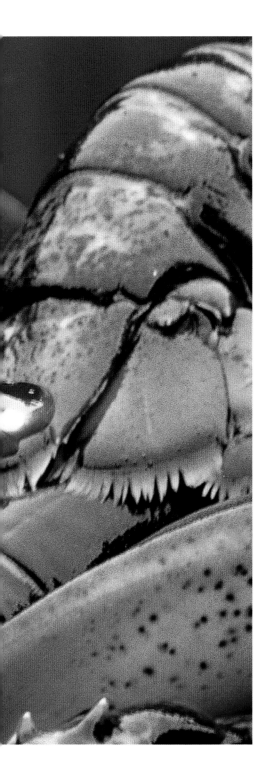

Already Framed

DEBORAH MURREN
NIKON 8008S, NIKKOR 70-300. FUJI FILM

A window frame makes a still life out
of shingles on the Belfast waterfront.

Two Old Tugs

WILLIAM MATTERN
CANON REBEL, AGRACHROME

Two old tugs wait to be called. Soon
they will tow someone up the river.

Mack Point

DEBORAH MURREN
NIKON 8008S, 70-300 NIKKOR AF,
FUJI VELVIA

Tugboats make a home in Belfast harbor where they are called on to pull or push barges up river as far as Bangor and Brewer.

(opposite)

**Sweepings from the
Harbor Floor**

TERESA C. POINDEXTER
SEA & SEA MM II EX, SENSIA ASA 50

Barnacles, rocks and seaweed mix
on the floor of Belfast harbor as the
tide approaches.

(above)

Starfish

DEBORAH MURREN
NIKON FM, NIKKOR 105MM, FUJI FILM

A starfish at Lincolnville Beach.

Quiet Beach Morning

DEBORAH MURREN
NIKON 8008S, NIKKOR 70-300, FUJI FILM

If a beach lover is early enough,
Lincolnville Beach can feel remote and
isolated. The beach is popular with
tourists and locals on warm summer
days and boasts an excellent seafood
eatery a short distance away.

Bridge Work

BRIANNE SEEKINS
CANON AE 1, FUJI FILM

Night drops its cover over the Belfast Bridge and the Passagassawakeag River, as it empties into Penobscot Bay.

Weskeag Sunset (*following page*)

ANNIE BURBANK
LEICA M-2, FUJI VELVIA

The sun sets over the Weskeag River in South Thomaston. The river flows into the Bay on the east side of the St. George Peninsula.

(above and opposite)

Seasonal Sun

TERESA DRINKWATER
PENTEX K1000

Belfast Harbor is lighted by a rising sun
on a pleasant September awakening,
but three months later, looks less invit-
ing as it awaits an incoming tide in
chilly December.

The Reservoir's Voice

CHRISTIE CAPUTO
CANON AUTOMATIC, FUJI 400

The Belfast Reservoir uses the lower
Congress Street Dam to make itself
heard on its way to the Bay. The reservoir is fed by the Little River and Piper
Stream, northwest of the town.

Running Tide (*above*)

GRETCHEN HESS GAGE
PENTEX ZX7, KODAK MAX 400

The tide shows signs of receding not far from the Belfast bridge.

Sleeping Fleet (*right*)

BRIANNE SEEKINS
CANON AE 1, FUJI FILM

Lobster boats, tugs and day sailing craft hover about in Belfast Harbor as the sun sets.

Misty Morning

GLORIA L. DAVIS
35 MM PENTEX

A June sun starts working its magic
over a morning mist on Sennebec
Lake in Appleton.

Evening, Belfast Harbor (*top*)

BRIANNE SEEKINS
CANON AE 1, FUJI FILM

The Belfast waterfront takes on an
extra dimension as city lights bounce
across the harbor.

Waiting for Daylight (*bottom*)

LINDA A. BUCKLIN
PENTEX 100, KODAK 200

The first light of dawn helps silhouette
boats at anchor in Belfast Harbor. The
Route One bridge in the background
shows no sign of the heavy traffic
to come.

Fall Foliage

GRETCHEN HESS GAGE
PENTEX ZX7, KODAK MAX 400

Foliage at its peak along the shores
of Pitcher Pond.

Angel and Epitaph

EMILY L. CROCKER (*above*)

DEBORAH MURRAN (*left*)
NIKON 8008, NIKKON 70-300MM, FUJI FILM

"Ye shall receive a crown of glory that fadeth not away," reads the epitaph contemplated by an angel in a Belfast cemetery.

A Shingle Mosaic

TERESA C. POINDEXTER
SEA & SEA MM II EX, SENSIA ASA 50

Worn by weather and creased by shadows, a wall of shingles at Charles and Park Streets in Belfast is turned into a medium for an art form.

Lupine Season *(opposite, top)*

MARCIA L. GEYER
CANON A-1, KODAK GOLD 100

A field off Prospect Road in Searsport comes alive with Lupine, a common flower along Maine roads and highways.

New Year's Trappings *(opposite, bottom)*

JEREMY MARDEN
CANON REBEL, KODAK 200

Like something the Roman's might have built, the bridge work at Duck Trap in Lincolnville faces a new millenium on New Year's morning, 2000.

Bloom Times

AMY CAMBELL (*above*)
NIKON

ANNIE BURBANK/IMAGEWRIGHT (*right*)
LEICA M-2, FUJI VELVIA

Apple trees in Lincolnville and South Thomaston are in full blossom on a June day. The heavy bloom usually signals a good crop by harvest time in late August and early September.

Moose Point Morning (*opposite*)

TERESA C. POINDEXTER
SEA & SEA MM II EX, SENSIA ASA 50

A side trail in Moose Point State Park is alive with springtime's lush greenery on an overcast morning.

Octoberfest (*above*)

MARCIA L. GEYER
CANON A-1, KODAK GOLD 100

October rises in triumph beside the shores of Swan Lake and Goose River in Belfast.

Autumn on Pitcher Pond (*left*)

MARCIA L. GEYER
CANON A-1, KODAK GOLD 100

Pitcher Pond might be renamed "Picture Pond" as it poses for a well-dressed portrait on a clear autumn day.

After all these years. . .

DEBORAH MURREN
NIKON 8008S, NIKKOR 70-300, FUJI FILM

A little the worse for its years of loyal service, a booth in a eatery in downtown Belfast basks in the morning light, awaiting the next customer.

Rockport's ancient lime kilns are a reminder of a crucial nineteenth century industry the town has all but forgotten. The kilns needed 30 cords of wood for burning off solidifying chemicals in limestone to produce a barrel of powdered lime.

The snug harbor, slightly rolling outer anchorage, and scores of amenities all allow Camden to play host to hundreds of yachts at a time.

Summer Portrait (*above*)

JEFFREY L. BOWMAN
NIKON N8008, KODAK EKTACHROME

Camden Harbor from the heights of
nearby Mt. Battie.

Season's End (*opposite*)

BILL MATTERN
CANON REBEL, AGFACHROME

By mid-fall, many of the windjammers
and schooners from Camden are in
the process of laying up for the winter.

Autumn Portrait (*above*)

AMY CAMPBELL
NIKON

This view of Camden Harbor in
October is one of the most spectacu-
lar on the Maine coast.

Sunset At Laite Beach (*opposite*)

JEFFREY L. BOWMAN
NIKON N8008, FUJICHROME SENSIA II

The morning stillness gives way to an
afternoon sailing breeze. The mid coast
of Maine is considered one of the
premier sailing areas in the world.

Waiting Dinghy (*above*)

AMY CAMPBELL
NIKON

If all the dinghies and all the wooden rowboats in all the harbors from Kittery to Calais were lashed end-to-end, how far would they stretch? At least from Port Clyde to Isle Au Haut.

Sitters Wanted (*left*)

JEFFREY L. BOWMAN
NIKON N8008, FUJICHROME SENSIA

A summer cottage porch in Northport awaits someone to occupy a rocking chair and watch the world pass by.

Dinghyville

AMY CAMPBELL
NIKON

These dinghies in Camden are used as commuters to vessels moored in the harbor. Wooden boats are cherished items along the coast, and are still built to traditional specifications.

Sea Life, II (*opposite, top*)

ANNIE BURBANK/IMAGEWRIGHT
LEICA M2, FUJI VELVIA

Another Maine fisherman goes about
making a living. Besides guiding the boat,
this job calls for baiting and dropping
traps, hauling and emptying others.

Great Good Fortune (*opposite, bottom*)

ANNIE BURBANK/IMAGEWRIGHT
LEICA M2, FUJI VELVIA

The pot of gold at the end of the
rainbow seems to be somewhere in
Camden-Rockport, or the jewel-like
countryside and seashore nearby.
Gold or not, it is a place of endless
beauty and fascination.

Signal Before Turning

PAULA JEAN LUNT
CANON, FUJI

From Kayaks to windjammers and
working fishing boats, Camden Harbor
is never at a loss for traffic coming,
going or idling.

Sea Life, I (*above*)

ANNIE BURBANK/IMAGEWRIGHT
LEICA M2, FUJI VELVIA

A captain at the helm guides his boat across the Bay in foul weather. The game is to control the sails and currents and avoid any number of mean ledges rising and falling with the tides.

Tenders (*right*)

MARNI LYN SIENKO
MINOLTA MAXXUM 400SI, KODAK

At the low end of the boat chain, a cluster of tenders await the return trip to their mother crafts moored in the harbor.

Faithful Friend (*opposite*)

MARNI LYN SIENKO
MINOLTA MAXXUM 400SI, KODAK

A fine example of wooden boating. These boats dotted Maine harbors until the advent of fiberglass construction. It is a wonderful sight.

Rockport Harbor

CYNTHIA LEWIS
CANON REBEL 2000, FUJI FILM 200

Rockport Harbor's south-facing V-shape entry makes it easy for sailing crafts to approach. The harbor has been greeting Europeans since before the Revolutionary War.

Day Sailing (right)

JEFFREY L. BOWMAN
NIKON N8008, KODAK EKTACHROME 100

Day sailing on Penobscot Bay provides passengers with a scenic perspective that is unmatched. For visitors looking for the experience, a number of commercial services are available.

Waterfront

CYNTHIA LEWIS
CANON REBEL 2000, FUJI FILM 200

Rockport's waterfront was once occupied by ice houses and lime kilns, many of which were eliminated in 1907 by a fire that started in a kiln, wiped out the ice houses, and spread to the rest of the village.

End of the Season (above)

BILL MATTERN
CANON REBEL, AGFACHROME

At season's end, windjammers and schooners head for warmer Florida waters or the Caribbean.

Curtis Island Light (left)

CAROLYN BEARCE
SEARS SLR 35, KODAK GOLD 200

Curtis Island Light stands north of Ogier Point at the entrance to Camden Harbor. It is one of eight lighthouses in Penobscot Bay.

Awaiting Departure (opposite)

CYNTHIA LEWIS
CANON REBEL 2000, FUJI FILM 200

The windjammer Mary Day sets at home in Camden Harbor. A number of windjammers gather at Camden and other Penobscot Bay harbors, taking passengers on weeklong sailing adventures along the Maine coast.

Harbor Reflections (*above*)

DEBORAH MURREN
NIKON FM, FUJI VELVIA

A still life with ripples, nature frequently and casually imitates art along a Penobscot Bay waterfront.

Andre's Home (*opposite*)

BILL MATTERN
CANON REBEL, AGFACHROME

The waterfront was the "homeport" for Andre the Seal, rescued by locals while injured. Andre gained world renown for his looks and personality.

Golden Sunset (*above*)

AMY CAMBELL
NIKON

The harbor basks in a sun set seen from Laite Beach.

Sunset, Aldermere Farm (*left*)

JEFFREY L. BOWMAN
NIKON N8008, FUJICHROME SENSIA II

The sun sets over Aldermere Farm looking east toward Penobscot Bay.

Frosty Oar Locks *(right)*

ANNIE BURBANK/IMAGEWRIGHT
LEICA M2, FUJI VELVIA

Winter has settled over the dock, but the work for dinghies and their heftier kin didn't go away with the passing of summer.

Sunrise *(below)*

JEFFREY L. BOWMAN
NIKON N8008, FUJICHROME SENSIA II

Dramatic lights, colors and cloud shapes provide subjects for photographers in the right place at the right time.

Lake Megunticook
(*opposite top and bottom*)

DEBORAH MURREN
NIKON N8008S, FUJI VELVIA

The sun sets over Lake Megunticook.

Laite Beach (*above*)

JEFFREY L. BOWMAN
NIKON N8008, FUJICHROME SENSIA II

A red sky at night will gladden the heart of sailors everywhere as the red sky in the morning gives good reasons for warning.

Schooners

ANNIE BURBANK/IMAGEWRIGHT
LEICA M2, FUJI VELVIA

The schooner *Surprise* is outward bound, while the *Olad* coasts home in a sunset.

Autumn Highlights

ANNIE BURBANK/IMAGEWRIGHT (*above*)
LEICA M2, FUJI VELVIA

AMY CAMPBELL (left and *opposite*)
NIKON

Blazing colors and reflections light
up autumn along the shores of
Megunticook Lake, the Megunticook
River at Shirt Tail Point in Camden,
and along Maple Allee off Union
Street in Rockport.

Becalmed (opposite)

AUDREY M. DEVENEY
YASHICA, KODAK GOLD

Seen from the deck of the *Angelique*, windjammers *Mercantile* and *Grace Bailey* idle away a still, foggy morning in Camden Harbor. In late June and July, warm, moist air in the so called Bermuda highs works toward the northeast and the cold waters off the Maine coast. The result can be days when fog banks roll inland at night and retreat just off the coast during the day.

Autumn Reflections (above)

ANN RACKLIFF
OLYMPIS OM-2000, KODAK GOLD 100

Mace Pond, near Camden is an absolute mirror for Mother Nature on a quiet autumn morning.

Rockport Harbor (*opposite*)

CYNTHIA LEWIS
CANON REBEL 2000, FUJI FILM 200

Much of Rockport Harbor has been transformed from the days when the cargo carriers came and went under sail. Today's park-like amenities and launching facilities make the harbor a favorite stop over and homeport to many boaters.

Nature's Fabrics (*top*)

DEBORAH MURREN
NIKON FM, FUJI SENSIA

Queen Anne's lace in a Rockport garden are the fabrics for a color show.

Wild Flower Slope (*bottom*)

AMY CAMPBELL
NIKON

A bee's view of a field in bloom on Bay View Street in Camden.

Quiet Perfection (*above*)

ANNIE BURBANK/IMAGEWRIGHT
LEICA M2, FUJI VELVIA

A Wyeth-like still life is an exercise in composition.

The Buckles Are Missing (*opposite*)

JOAN PICCARD
OLYMPUS OM-25, KODAK 200

Belted Galloways, easily recognized by passersby in the Camden-Rockport area, contentedly munch away in a morning fog. The Galloways were originally a breed of all black Scottish beef cattle. The belts came later.

Seasonal Gowns (above)

ELIZABETH CROCKETT
PENTEX, KODAK

The Megunticook River near
Washington Street in Camden is
gowned in October glory.

Glen Cove (left)

PENNY SANBORN
CANON REBEL X EOS, KODAK 400

Glen Cove from along Route One
shines on a late summer afternoon.
Originally called Clam Cove, the
first settlers to these shores arrived
in 1781.

Autumn Bouquet

JOHN D. WILLIAMS
NIKON 6006, KODAK GOLD 100

A view of South Thomaston from
Route One is framed by a bouquet of
fall colors that appear freshly applied.

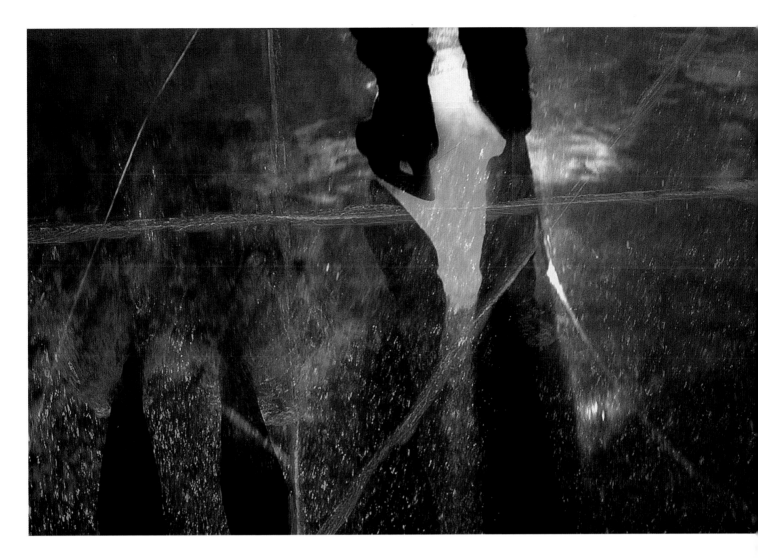

Winter Woods (*opposite*)

ELIZABETH CROCKETT
PENTEX, KODAK

The woods along the Megunticook
River have changed their dress to a
lacy white.

CROSSING T's (*above*)

ANNIE BURBANK/IMAGEWRIGHT
LEICA M2, FUJI VELVIA

A Rockland quarry provides a surface
for some deep winter figures practice.

Owls Head Lighthouse is located above Munroe Island on the south side of Rockland Harbor.

Although it looks like a hodgepodge of islands, Muscle Ridge Channel is a safe, easy passageway to Rockland (top left) and Penobscot Bay. Tenants Harbor is in the foreground.

Schooner Days: Remembrance of Things Past

(*above*)
PAUL JEAN LUNT
CANON EOS A2, FUJI 100

(*left and opposite*)
ANNIE BURBANK/IMAGEWRIGHT
LEICA M-2, FUJI VELVIA

Penobscot Bay Schooner Days is a celebration of the ships that were first built in the bay in 1791 and which became the standard working vessel for marine commerce along the east coast until the second half of the 19th century. Today the boats come in various lengths and modifications—and prices—but still demand accomplished sailors and helmsmen. The Heritage is under full sail coming right at the photographer's lens, while Surprise is outward bound. The schooners use a number of Penobscot harbors during the celebration.

Two Ketches and a Fair Breeze

ANNIE BURBANK/IMAGEWRIGHT
LEICA M-2, FUJI VELVIA

Perhaps the only thing better than a
fair breeze and a full sail is another
boat to race against, as this pair of
ketches seems to be doing during a
perfect Penobscot day.

Clear Day, Clear Course

ANNIE BURBANK/IMAGEWRIGHT
LEICA M-2, FUJI VELVIA

Ice sailing attracts a squadron of winter
sailors on the surface of Chickawaukie
Pond, north of Rockland.

Where The Ocean Meets The Wall

(above asnd opposite)

PENNY SANBORN (opposite and above)
CANON REBEL XEOS, KODAK GOLD 200

(right)

LOUIS M. DELENA
PENTEX IQ ZOOM 160,
KODAK GOLD 200

Rockland harbor provides shelter and parking spaces for a variety of sea-going traffic. It is one of the busiest working harbors north of Portland. The historic 4,200 foot Rockland Break-water with its light house, was built with granite cut from nearby island quarries. The wall is also a tribute to Rockland's place as the granite-shipping capital of the world in the late 19th century. The breakwater saved boats as well as wharves from eastern storms.

(opposite)

Scaring Away The Pirates (top)

JOAN R. PICCARD
OLYMPUS OM-2S, KODAK 200

A pair of jack-o-lanterns keep watch over the *J & E Riggins* deck as the Rockland-based boat stands at anchor in the thoroughfare between Vinalhaven and North Haven.

Show Offs (bottom)

MARY BONINA
CANON SURE SHOT, KODAK GOLD 200

The Kermit Chorus hold forth at the annual Lobster Festival in Rockland.

The Kitchen Queen (opposite)

ANNIE BURBANK/IMAGEWRIGHT
LEICA M-2, FUJI VELVIA

The intrepid cookstove, the traditional center of life in the 19th century household, has become a much-sought-after antique in the present day. As a photographer's "model," it serves as an impressive still life, whether hot or cold.

The Day's Work (*top and bottom*)

PAULA JEAN LUNT
CANON EOS A2, FUJI 100

A sternman sets the bait for another trap, while later in the day, back at Tenants Harbor, a fisherman secures the mooring line.

Sunset at Owls Head

ANNIE BURBANK/IMAGEWRIGHT
LEICA M2, FUJI VELVIA

At Owls Head, a dory awaits a calling.

Owls Head Light (*top*)

PAULA JEAN LUNT
CANON EOS A2, FUJI 100

Snow and sky frame Owls Head lighthouse located above Munroe Island on the south side of Rockland Harbor.

Tenants Harbor (bottom and *opposite*)

BILL MATTERN
CANON REBEL, AGFACHROME 100

One of the busy and picturesque ports on the bay, Tenants Harbor is tucked well in from Two Bush Channel.

Looking For Mouse (*above*)

JAMES BALDOCCHI
LEICA M4, KODAK GOLD 100

A pleasure boat leaves Tenants Harbor in a fog on its way to Mouse Island.

Heading Home (*right*)

BILL MATTERN
CANON REBEL, AGFACHROME

After a day on the bay, a schooner rounds Owls Head on its way home to Rockland Harbor.

Nature's Violins (*opposite*)

ANNIE BURBANK/IMAGEWRIGHT
LEICA M2, FUJI VELVIA

Fiddlehead ferns stand tightly tuned along a roadside in Tenants Harbor. A traditional delicacy, edible fiddleheads have a short season, requiring harvesting before they mature in the first warm days of summer.

Blurry Start (top and bottom)

DEBORAH MURREN
NIKON FM, FUJI VELVIA

Fishermen at Owls Head prepare for
work despite a heavy fog. The fog has
to lift high enough from the water surface so that buoys can be seen.

Remains of The Day (opposite)

ANNIE BURBANK/IMAGEWRIGHT
LEICA M2, FUJI VELVIA

A summer day has its own pace as the
tide comes and goes before the sun
finally sets over Ballyhac Cove.

Ballyhac Cove (*above*)

ANNIE BURBANK/IMAGEWRIGHT
LEICA M2, FUJI VELVIA

Peaceful and solitary, Ballyhac Cove awaits a visitor who will drop anchor for the night.

Bar Island (*opposite, top*)

PAULA JEAN LUNT
CANON EOS A2, FUJI 50

The sun sets over Bar Island off Spruce Head. It is about a mile from Spruce Head to Whitehead Island Light at the southwest edge of the Muscle Ridge Channel leading to Owls Head and Rockland. The Muscle Ridge Islands are a favorite overnight stop for yachtsmen.

Hart's Neck (*opposite, bottom*)

MARY BONINA
CANON SURE SHOT 85 ZOOM, KODAK GOLD 200

A summer morning sunrise from Hart's Neck, overlooking Tenants Harbor.

A Nip in The Air (*above*)

PAULA JEAN LUNT
CANON EOS A2, FUJI 100

Testimony to the zero temperature of a winter morning on the water is the so called "artic fog" engulfing fishermen heading off to tend their traps.

Home Gallery (*left*)

EMILY G. LOWE
GRAPHFLEX, PORTRA 160 VC

A dining room wall serves as a gallery in the West Rockport home where the photographer grew up.

Twin Dinks

DEBORAH MURREN
NIKON FM, FUJI VELVIA

At dockside, a brace of dinghies await
the call for a return to crafts at their
moorings.

Dockside Lunch

CYNTHIA LEWIS
CANON REBEL 2000, FUJI FILM 200

At dockside on a summer day, tourists
can take lunch at the water's edge.

Owls Head Light (*top*)

IRENEUS C. WEYMOUTH
PENTEX 140, KODAK MAX 40

Built of white granite in 1826, Owls
Head Light guides boat traffic into the
south end of Rockland Harbor.

Snug Harbor (*bottom*)

KIMBERLEE BRETTA
PENTEX 35/300, FUJI FILM

The entrance to Tenants Harbor is
protected by three small islands.

Lobster Boat

CYNTHIA LEWIS
CANON REBEL 2000, FUJI FILM 200

Tenants Harbor is a busy fishing village with lobstermen loading for the day's work and returning with their catches. Their buoys and traps area a common sight at dockside.

Climbers (*top*)

JOAN HARJULA
MINOLTA FREEDOM, KODAK GOLD 200

Waterman's Beach in South
Thomaston, on a day when sun, snow
and sky complement a cottage
owner's collection of "climbing buoys."

Sign Posts (*bottom*)

CAROLYN BEARCE
SEARS SLR, KODAK GOLD 200

Buoys, the sign posts and signatures of
the lobster business, await a match-up
with traps stacked outside an Owls
Head fish house.

Port Clyde enjoys an easy harmony between working fishermen and recreational boating enthusiasts. The Port Clyde General Store wharf, where yachtsmen are welcome to tie up, is also a temporary storage area for thousands of lobster traps.

The best anchorage in Port Clyde is in its eastern coves, which afford easy access to the accomodating town. The approaches are studded by thousands of lobsterpots—jewels to the eye, hazards to the propeller.

Dock Days *(above)*

BILL MATTERN
CANON REBEL, AGFACHROME 100

A load of lobster traps and buoys on a dock at Port Clyde await a chance to go back to work.

Beacon at Marshall Point *(left)*

PAULA JEAN LUNT
CANON A-2, FUJI 100

The light at Marshall Point guides homeboats approaching Port Clyde harbor from the south.

ME 391A *(opposite)*

MARCIA L. GEYER
CANON 1-A, KODAK GOLD 100

With fisherman setting and hauling as many as 1,000 traps each, stacking space can be a at a premium.

The Knight's Tale (*top*)

BILL MATTERN
CANON REBEL, AGFACHROME 100

St. George encounters his nemesis in front of the town hall that bears his name.

Fog Bell (*bottom*)

BILL MATTERN
CANON REBEL, AGFACHROME

The Monhegan Mailboat, as it is known, uses the light and Hart Island as guideposts on its 22-mile round trip back and forth to the harbor.

Retired Anchor

BILL MATTERN
CANON REBEL, AGFACHROME

To the west of Marshall Point is
Hooper Island, to the east, a series of
islands ledges known as The Brothers.

The Essentials (*top*)

AMY CAMPBELL
NIKON

Traps and buoys await boat and bait
along the waterfront at Port Clyde.

Marshall Point Light (*bottom*)

BILL MATTERN
CANON REBEL, AGFACHROME

The lighthouse, originally built in 1823,
stands 30 feet high. It was rebuilt in
1858.

Traps On Standby (above)

BILL MATTERN
CANON REBEL, AGFACHROME 100

Time and tide may wait for no man.
Lobster traps, on the other hand, seem
to always be waiting. A formidable
collection dries in the sun on a Port
Clyde dock before moving on to its
next resting place in a darker,
damper world.

Night Light (right)

DEBORAH MURREN
NIKON 8008S, FUJI VELVIA

A lantern on a Port Clyde dock does
its best against the gathering darkness.

Cutting The Fog (above)

JEFFREY L. BOWMAN
NIKON N8008, FUJICHROME

Like a candle in the dark, the lamp atop the Marshall Point Lighthouse cuts through the fog on a bad day for Penobscot boatmen.

Growing Season (left)

ANNIE BURBANK/IMAGEWRIGHT
LEICA M-2, FUJI VELVIA

Summer on the St. George Peninsula comes alive with shapes and colors, from hay fields to flower gradens and wildflowers along the roadways.

The Other Side (opposite)

AMY CAMPBELL
NIKON

The porch behind the Ocean House at Port Clyde, a side of town not many people get around to seeing.

Full Canvas

JOANNE E. BARKSDALE
CANON EOS REBEL, KODAK GOLD 200

The Victory Chimes, under full sail,
rounds Marshall Point Light heading
for Port Clyde.

Nesting Place

PAMELA SWING
NIKON FM, KODAK GOLD 100

Mother Earth keeps an egg tucked
among boulders near Marshall Point.
The boulders are remains from the
passage of the last glacier. The "egg"
probably washed in on a storm-
driven tide.

Snow Covered Traps (top)

PAULA JEAN LUNT
CANON EOS A 2, FUJI 100

Lobster pots under a blanket of snow.
This collection is in storage for a few
more weeks.

Mosquito Sunrise (bottom)

AMY CAMPBELL
NIKON

Morning appears over Mosquito Head
Beach near Martinville on the bay side
of the St. George Peninsula.

Haying in Hope, Maine

ANNIE BURBANK/IMAGEWRIGHT
LEICA M-2, FUJI VELVIA

A rite of summer, the haying season takes place in early to mid July and, if conditions are favorable, a second crop can be cut by early fall. Instead of the laborious chore once faced by rural families with livestock to feed, haying has become a specialty of a few contractors with cutting and bailing equipment.

(*above and opposite*)

We'll Catch The Next One

CYNTHIA LEWIS
CANON EOS REBEL, KODAK 200

The Monhegan mail boat, with passengers and supplies, passes the Port Clyde waterfront on its way to the island. The village general store offers a popular outdoor waiting room for passengers coming or going.

Channel Sentry (*right*)

JOHN P. FEERICK
MINOLTA MAXXUM 51, KODAK MAX 400

The Marshall Point Light guards the Port Clyde channel looking westward toward Hooper Island.

Visitors to the Monhegan Island Hotel usually fill the old landmark to capacity in July and August.

More than 400 species of wildflowers grow on Monhegan Island. Monhegan Island mixes lobstermen and artists with a strong dose of tourists, coming out no worse for the wear.

Wide Open (*above*)

ANNIE BURBANK/IMAGEWRIGHT
LEICA M-2, FUJI VELVIA

A racer off Vinalhaven puts his boat to the test. Some ports along the Maine coast stage summer lobsterboat races, a diversion requiring real working boats with large in-board engines, and considerable prize money. It is best to perform in waters that are unobstructed by ledges or shoals. Seat belts and anchors aren't required.

Morning Fog (*left*)

AMY CAMPBELL
NIKON

A morning fog can slow the pace of summer life around Monhegan Harbor, and at only 200 feet above sea level, there is no place to rise above it all.

Green Island (*opposite*)

ANNIE BURBANK/IMAGEWRIGHT
LEICA M-2, FUJI VELVIA

Green Island sets off the east shore of Vinalhaven, one of a half dozen islets facing Isle Au Haut and the Saddleback Ledge Light.

Meeting At Matinicus (*above*)

CYNTHIA LEWIS
CANON EOS, FUJI 200

Matinicus Harbor, about 15 miles by ferry from Rockland, is a busy summer lobstering port that's also an overnight anchorage for pleasure boats plying the outer reachings of the Bay.

Title (*left*)

AMY CAMPBELL
NIKON

A garden in front of the Monhegan Island Inn contibutes to the 600 botantical species found on the island.

Title (*above*)

AMY CAMPBELL
NIKON

A show of hands along a fence appear about to applaud the sun.

Island Charm (*right*)

PAULA JEAN LUNT

A front porch and a slat fence frame the front yard of a Vinalhaven home. Island and coastal homes, especially those that are pre-20th century, have become premium properties in the Penobscot Bay area.

Monhegan Summer (*above*)

CYNTHIA LEWIS
CANON EOS, FUJI 200

Summer visitors to the Monhegan Island Hotel usually fill the old landmark to capacity. In July and August, lobsterboats are found beached for repairs.

Island View (*right*)

PAMELA SWING
NIKON FM, KODAK ROYAL GOLD

For more than a century, Monhegan has been home to a colony of artists who arrive each June for a three-month stay. The most prominent of the present generation is Jamie Wyeth.

Princess (*above*)

CYNTHIA LEWIS
CANON EOS, FUJI 200

Lobstermen converge at Matinicus Harbor after a day's work. Matinicus Rock Light is about five miles south beyond Criehaven and Ragged Island.

Haul Out (*left*)

CYNTHIA LEWIS
CANON EOS, FUJI 200

Unlike most Maine lobster ports, Monhegan's season runs from January to late June, for island residents only. They set about 1,000 traps per fisherman.

Yawl at Ease (*left*)

CYNTHIA LEWIS
CANON EOS, FUJI 200

A favorite of coastal sailors, the Yawl design usually runs under sail when clear of the harbor. It becomes more maneuverable by switching to its engine when in waterfront traffic or close channels.

Matinicus Sunrise (*below*)

CYNTHIA LEWIS
CANON EOS, FUJI 200

A roost of seagulls watch a pinpoint of rising sunlight as it pokes above the eastern finger of Matinicus Harbor at one of the quietest times of the day.

Pulpit Harbor Fog (*opposite*)

CYNTHIA LEWIS
CANON 2000, FUJI 2000

The month of July is the foggiest along the Maine coast, with the great gray of an elephant rolling in on one occasion, and sneaking up on Sandburg's little cat feet the next. Either way, it's best to be in harbor when it arrives.

Low Tide (*above*)

PAMELA SWING
NIKON FM, KODAK ROYAL GOLD

Along the shores of Monhegan, an artist's eye might pick out this ancient sea goddess with her sea weed hair, neck and shoulders rising from the sea.

Life on The Bottom (*left*)

THERESA C. POINDEXTER
SEA & SEA MMII, SENSIA ASA 50

The underwater community off Monheagn Island is caught 20 feet down in 53 degree water with the aid of a YS-120 strobe light.

Safe in The Pulpit (*opposite*)

CYNTHIA LEWIS
CANON 2000, FUJI 2000

Fog foils sailing traffic around the Bay, leaving skippers to wait out the weather in cozy Pulpit Harbor on the north shore of North Haven Island.

Shore Delights *(above and opposite)*

PAMELA SWING
NIKON FM, KODAK ROYAL GOLD

Anna finds a lifetime of wonders amid
the sand and boulders of her
Penobscot Bay sea shore.

CONTRIBUTORS

James Baldocchi
5413 Belgrave Place
Oakland, CA 94618
87

Joanne E. Barksdale
Harrington Cove Road
HCR33 Box 388
Spruce Head, ME 04859
108

Carolyn Bearce
18 Tilden Road
Scituate, MA 02066
50, 97

Mary Bonina
44 Thingvalla Avenue
Cambridge, MA 02138
80, 91

Jeffrey L. Bowman
34 Pearl Street
Camden, ME 04843
38, 41, 42, 48, 54, 55, 57, 106

Kimberlee Bretta
HC35 80 Box 771
Tenants Harbor, ME 04860
95

Linda Bucklin
HCR 80 Box 23
Belfast, ME 04915
27

Annie Burbank
Imagewright
Box 914
Rockport, ME 04856
*Cover, 6, 20–21, 33, 44 (2), 47,
55, 59, 60, 71, 74, 75, 76, 77,
81, 83, 86, 89, 90, 106, 111,
116, 117*

Amy Campbell
Box 659
Rockport, ME 04856
*33, 40, 42, 43, 54, 60, 61, 65, 104,
107, 110, 116, 118, 119*

Christie Caputo
RR2 Box 2188
Belfast, ME 04915
24

Elizabeth Crockett
P.O. Box 1123
Camden, ME 04843
68, 70

Emily Crooker
16 Stover Lane
Belfast, ME 04915
29 (2)

Gloria Davis
555 West Street
Rockport, ME 04856
26

Louis DeLena
16 Forest Court
Malden, MA 02148
79

Audrey M. Deveney
P.O. Box 936
Belfast, ME 04915
62

Teresa Drinkwater
RR1 Box 1496
Stockton Springs, ME 04981
22, 23

John P. Feerick
412 Hale Street
Prides Crossing, MA 01965
113

Marcia L. Geyer
P.O. Box 1199
Belfast, ME 04915
30, 34 (2), 101

Joan Harjula
74 Hyler Street
Thomaston, ME 04861
97

Gretchen Hess Gage
119 Cedar Street
Belfast, ME 04915
25, 28

Cynthia Lewis
51a Kent Street
Newburyport, MA 01950
*48, 49, 51, 64, 94, 96, 112, 113,
118, 120, 121 (2), 122)2), 123, 125*

Emily G. Lowe
P.O. Box 96
West Rockport, ME 04865
92

Paula Jean Lunt
Lunt Studio
P.O. Box 295
Tenants Harbor, ME 04860
*8, 45, 74, 82 (2), 84, 91, 92,
100, 110, 119*

Jeremy Marden
RR 4 Box 4165
Lincolnville, ME 04849
30

Bill Mattern
429 Country Way
Scituate, MA 02066
*14, 39, 50, 53, 84, 85, 87, 100,
102 (2), 103, 104, 105*

Deborah Murren
P.O. Box 5
Batesville, VA 22924
*9, 12, 13, 15, 17, 18, 35, 52,
56 (2), 65, 88 (2), 93, 105*

Poan R. Piccard
Box 1404
Camden, ME 04843
67, 80

Teresa C. Poindexter
41 Grove Street #2
Belfast, ME 04915
16, 31, 32, 124

Ann Rackliff
27 Florence Street
Rockland, ME 04841
63

Penny Sanborn
332 Beechwood Street
Thomaston, ME 04861
68, 78, 79

Brianne Seekins
RR4 Box 2609
Belfast, ME 04915
19, 25, 27

Marni Lyn Sienko
12 Main Street #3
Camden, ME 04843
46, 47

Pamela Swing
54 Frances Street
Concord, MA 01742
109, 120, 124, 126, 127

Ireneus C. Weymouth
728 Glen Oaks Drive
Leesburg, FL 34748
95

John D. Williams
6 Gale Avenue
Rockport, MA 01966
69